# Bike E

## Top tips and expert advice
## for the new cyclist

**by Peter Andrews**

## eco-logic books

First Published in 2008 by
eco-logic books
Mulberry House, 19 Maple Grove, Bath BA2 3AF
www.eco-logicbooks.com

Illustrations © Susanna Kendall

ISBN 978-1899233175

Illustrations by Susanna Kendall
Editing by Alethea Doran
Book and Cover Design by Steve Palmer, The Design Co-operative
Printed and bound in the UK by www.russellpress.com
Printed on de-inked post consumer waste – this book is fully compostable.

Further copies of the book may be ordered from eco-logic books. They also sell,
by mail order, books that promote practical solutions to environmental
problems, organic gardening, sustainable development, permaculture, peak oil,
transport and related topics.
Visit their web site at www.eco-logicbooks.com for a complete list.

The Small Print
Whilst every effort has been made to ensure the accuracy of the information in this book
the publisher and author accept no responsibility for any errors or omissions.

# Contents

# Introduction

This book explains how to buy the right bike and how to get truly comfortable riding it. It will send you off on relaxing rides in beautiful countryside and prepare you for the more serious business of cycle commuting. It covers kids' bikes, cycling clothes, security and how to carry loads by bike. It explains the principles of cycling safely and pleasurably on today's busy roads, and it introduces you to the basics of bike maintenance. With all that under your belt you'll be a confident, skilful, knowledgeable cyclist, and the world's roads, tracks, trails and cycle paths will be your personal pleasure ground.

As well as Bike Easy the book, there's the website, **www.bike-easy.org.uk**, with clickable links to a multitude of organisations, products and services. It provides additional tips for better biking and a forum through which you can comment, ask questions and share your own tips.

How you approach this book is up to you. If you're in a methodical mood, start at tip number 1 and work your way through to the end. Or, simply dip in and out as the fancy takes you. If there's a particular topic that interests you, go there first and spend time exploring it. You're in control of the journey – just as you are when you ride a bike.

# 1: Buying a bike

There are a number of different types of bike, each made for a specific purpose. To the uninitiated they all look pretty similar, but there are significant differences between them.

**Mountain bikes** are the 4x4s of the cycling world. They're extremely strong and are at their best on rough terrain. On tarmac roads they can feel sluggish compared with lighter bikes.

- Front and sometimes rear suspension
- Thick tubing
- Chunky tyres
- Powerful brakes
- Straight handlebars with bar ends
- Y-shaped frame
- No mudguards
- Up to 30 gears

**Racing bikes**, or **road bikes**, are cycling's greyhounds. The ride can be on the harsh side and you can feel rather squashed up. Racers are delicate creatures, easily damaged if you charge through potholes or off a kerb.

- Slender tubes
- Carbon-fibre fork
- Narrow wheels
- Smooth tyres
- Handlebars enable the rider to adopt a dropped-down, aerodynamic position

**Hybrids** combine the toughness and comfort of a mountain bike with the agility and lightness of a road bike. They make good general-purpose bikes, fine around town but equally at home on dirt trails and cycle tracks.

- Curved handlebars more comfortable to grip
- Mudguards
- Luggage rack
- Tyres smooth in the middle (for riding on-road) with knobbly edges (for off-road grip)

**City bikes** are another mix of mountain bike and road bike. They're intended for sedate urban cycling over relatively short distances.

- Upright riding position
- Soft saddle
- Mudguards
- Step-through frame
- Gears inside the rear wheel hub

**Touring bikes** are mechanical packhorses. There's some resemblance to a racing bike, but a tourer is many times stronger and much more comfortable whether you're spinning up the High Street or exploring the Great Silk Road.

- Dropped handlebars allow the rider to hold on in different positions, reducing fatigue
- Cages to hold water bottles
- Strong racks for panniers
- Wide range of gears
- Comfy saddle
- Mudguards

In addition to these types there are also expedition or trekking bikes, cruiser bikes, roadsters, folders, recumbent cycles, tandems and tricycles, as well as some truly weird stuff made by specialist manufacturers. Furthermore, all these different categories tend to be somewhat fluid, as manufacturers delight in blurring the boundaries – by marketing machines as urban mountain bikes, or fast tourers, for example – and they have a habit of claiming every new model to be revolutionary and radically different. So it can all be rather confusing.

The key to making the right choice is to think carefully about the sort of cycling you intend to do. Evaluate as many different bikes as you can, by reading reviews and road tests in bike magazines, and taking advice from other cyclists. Then, go for it!

Compared with life's other major purchases, such as houses, cars, holidays and domestic appliances, bicycles are unbeatable value. A bike will delight you, it will help keep you slim and healthy, and if you use it for day-to-day transport it will pay for itself in less than a year.

So once you've got some firm ideas it's time to visit cycle shops to discuss your requirements and to try some bikes.

**1: Buy from a bike shop.** You can buy a bike from car accessory stores, mail-order catalogues, toy shops, supermarkets and even some garden centres. Adverts appear from time to time offering bikes for as little as £50. Buy from these places and you will certainly get a machine with two wheels, handlebars and a saddle. But be warned: the bike will probably be heavy and poorly made, and components such as brakes and gears will be difficult if not impossible to adjust. It will arrive in a box for you to assemble, or it will have been thrown together by a bored shop assistant.

In an age when most independent shops have been replaced by chain stores, there is still a refreshing diversity of cycle retailer. These shops survive, indeed thrive, because they know their job. A bike from a proper cycle shop will cost you more than one from a cheapo outlet, but you will be buying a better product; plus, at no extra charge, precious expertise and support.

**2: Shop around.** Most bike shops purport to do everything, but in practice they often specialise, or at least lean towards, one or two particular types of cycling. It could be road racing, or mountain biking, or perhaps commuter bikes. Different shops also target different sections of the market: some will be at the cheap-and-cheerful end; others will specialise in high-tech wizardry with a price tag to match.

As well as checking out the bikes, take a look at the staff and other customers and assess the general ambience of the shop. If it sells off-road bikes and there are mud-spattered mountain bikers heatedly discussing the virtues of titanium seat pins with an impassioned shop assistant, that's probably a good sign. If there are leaflets promoting cycling organisations, or a noticeboard bristling with recent press cuttings and flyers advertising local cycling events, that also suggests that you're in a place that cares about cycling.

**3: Spend.** For about £150 you'll get a plain, no-frills bike. It may possibly have mudguards and a luggage rack. If not, these – along with accessories such as a lock, lights, luggage and a pump, plus any upgrades such as a better saddle – will all cost extra. So, be prepared to pay at least £200 for the total package. If you're on a tight budget and even £200 is beyond your reach, forget about buying brand new and go for a used bike (see Tips 8 and 9).

Spend more if you possibly can – think of it as an investment. £500 will buy you a bike that's noticeably lighter and with better-quality components. It'll be easier to ride, more reliable and last longer.

**4: Keep it simple.** If you're buying a bike for £150 or so, don't choose one with front and rear suspension and disc brakes. It may look like a top-notch mountain bike but it's faking it – those whizzy components are pale imitations of the real things. They will be badly made, poorly assembled and hard to repair: all they'll really add is a lot of weight (which forces you to pedal harder).

**5: Buy on a weekday.** Weekends are busy times for bike shops, and staff can be pressed for time. (Avoid Monday mornings too – few of us are at our best then.) Outside those times you should find a calmer atmosphere and people who are happy to talk and – more importantly – to listen to you. They will take time to assess your needs and will explain what bikes and related products they're able to provide. Salespeople who demonstrate things rather than just describe them are more likely to know their stuff.

**6: Expect good service**. Shops with staff who are anything less than polite, patient and obliging should be avoided. Very, very occasionally a town has a gem of a bike shop run by a curmudgeonly old genius whose knowledge and skills are priceless, and it may be worth tolerating a certain gruff eccentricity from such a person if they truly are the Stradivari of the cycling world. But, in general, if you encounter people who sneer at the idea of a bike to ride only on cycle tracks, or speak only techno-babble, or barely speak to you at all… take your business elsewhere.

**7: Try before you buy.** Once you're beyond browsing, ask to take two or three bikes for a test ride. Good cycle shops will encourage you to do this (although they may not have the bikes all set up and ready to ride, in which case your road tests will have to be scheduled for another day). The shop will also want some guarantee that you and the bike are going to reappear, so they'll ask for a deposit. A credit card swipe is usually sufficient.

Take the bike somewhere quiet and get a feel for how it fits (see Chapter 2), rides and responds. Are the handlebars the right height and shape? Does the bike corner easily? Is the ride smooth or sharp? Are the brakes soft or fierce? Do the gears change smoothly? (Though bear in mind that gear changing requires a light touch – duff changes might be down to you, rather than the bike). Even a short ride will reveal important differences and help you to make an informed choice.

**8: Buy online.** On a wild whim I once bought a big load-carrying bike like the ones used by the Royal Mail. It was a handsome beast, but I barely rode it and it was cluttering up the place, so I advertised it on eBay. It cost me £450 and I sold it for £300. Someone got an absolute bargain. So eBay has great potential – if you know what you're looking for. There are several points in its favour. You get to see pictures of the advertised bike and there's a much fuller description than in a newspaper or magazine ad. You can email questions to the seller or forward the information to knowledgeable friends for their opinion. The eBay feedback system enables you to get an idea of the seller's probity and reduces the risk of being sold dodgy goods.

The downside is that you don't get a chance to try the bike before buying it. You will also have to pay for delivery or collect the bike yourself. Or, if the bike is stripped down, boxed up and dispatched by a courier, you'll have to reassemble it.

**9**: **Buy ex-hire.** In the autumn and winter many cycle-hire businesses sell off some of their older bikes (although 'older' is a relative term: it might only mean last year's model) and there are often bargains to be had. The bikes may be a bit scuffed and scratched, but hire centres tend to run strong, reliable machines and they will have been well maintained. Find a hire business and chat up the proprietor.

**10**: **Check out the folding stuff.** Folding bikes are relatively expensive: from £400 to over £1,000 for top-of-the-range models from market leaders Brompton, Dahon and Birdy. They're more complex than normal bikes, so spares and repairs can be costly too. Folders are also something of a compromise when you come to ride them: the cheaper models have a limited range of gears, which means hills can be a struggle, and they don't cover distances as effortlessly as big-wheeled bikes can.

That said, folders have many advantages. They make it possible to combine a car or train journey with a bike ride, and when you reach your destination they can be collapsed and stowed away in a tiny space. The legendary Brompton bicycle is more space efficient than a Yorkshire terrier, and has the bonus that it won't chew your slippers. For city dwellers and commuters, making mainly short trips, a folding bike is well worth considering.

# 2: Sitting comfortably

Kids generally take to cycling pretty quickly, but for adults it may be a while before you're truly comfortable. If you're new to cycling, or coming back to it after a gap of several years, ease yourself into it gently. Go on short rides that end long before discomfort sets in. Wearing the right sort of clothing (see Chapter 3) can make a big difference too.

Comfort is also about setting the bike up properly and making adjustments and alterations where necessary. Just about everything on a bike can be fine-tuned or swapped for something better. Whatever your shape, size or riding style, with perseverance and patience you can achieve a perfect fit. Eventually, hopping on your bike will feel as natural and as comfortable as slipping into a well-worn pair of walking shoes.

**11: Size matters.** Buy a bike that's too small and you'll be squashed up with bits of you colliding with bits of the bike. Buy one that's too big and you won't be able to control the thing properly.

Straddle the bike of your choice and stand with both feet flat on the floor. There should be at least an inch (25mm) of clearance between your crotch and the top tube or crossbar. You'll want more clearance if it's a mountain bike and you plan to go bounding about off road, as there's a lot at risk!

With someone holding the bike upright, sit on the saddle and place the ball of each foot (that's the part between your toes and the arch) on the pedals. Pedal backwards slowly. When your foot is at the bottom of the pedal stroke your knee should be slightly bent. You should also be able to slide off the saddle and put both feet to the floor.

Do some more reverse pedalling and now try squeezing the brakes and reaching for the gear controls. You may have to lean forward slightly, but you shouldn't have to stretch.

**12: Sex matters.** As well as coming in different sizes, bikes are sometimes made gender-specific. Women generally have slightly shorter arms and torsos than men, and female bike frames are proportioned accordingly, making them more comfortable for women to ride.

Women's bikes often have a sloping crossbar or top tube, on the basis that such a design will be more decorous to ride when wearing a flowing skirt. The drawback is that 'open' frames of this kind tend to be weaker and heavier than conventional frames. For this reason, many women opt for a closed or 'man's' frame.

**13: Adjust.** Once you start using your new bike you're likely to discover that the fit falls just short of perfection. That's easily sorted with a few adjustments and maybe one or two replacements (see Tip 14).

## A few adjustments

**Saddle.** Your saddle has a surprising degree of adjustment potential. Set it to what feels like the right position and then go for a short ride, stopping to make further finer adjustments as necessary.

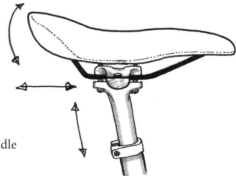

- **Height.** Pull the quick-release lever open, or slacken off the seatpost bolt. Move the post up or down. Take care not to exceed the maximum extension mark.
- **Reach.** Release the bolt underneath the saddle to slide it back or forward.
- **Tilt.** You can even adjust the tilt of the saddle slightly if you wish.

**Handlebars**. Your comfort may be improved by altering the height of your handlebars. Bars set too low can mean aching arms and a stiff neck. Too high and it can be difficult to pedal properly.

- **Headset Allen bolt**. Undo this to move your handlebars up or down by a couple of inches. Take care not to exceed the maximum extension mark.
- **Variable stem**. Often fitted to city bikes and hybrids, this is easily adjustable without the use of tools.
- **'Aheadset'**. Bikes with this sort of handlebar mounting can't be adjusted. If you need more height or reach, consider substituting different handlebars (See Tip 14).

**Brakes**. It should be easy to reach and operate your bike's brakes.

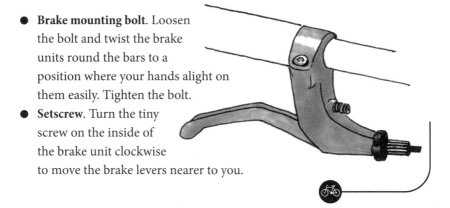

- **Brake mounting bolt**. Loosen the bolt and twist the brake units round the bars to a position where your hands alight on them easily. Tighten the bolt.
- **Setscrew**. Turn the tiny screw on the inside of the brake unit clockwise to move the brake levers nearer to you.

**14**: **Replace**. When you buy a car or a laptop or a dishwasher, you are buying an integrated unit and have to take what you are given. But with a bicycle you're in control: if any component meets with your displeasure you can usually swap it for something better. Even simple changes will alter the bike's feel and performance considerably.

## A few repalcements

**Saddle**. Bike makers know that saddles are a matter of personal choice and so most fit a cheap, foam-filled saddles as standard, expecting you to replace it. There are various types you may wish to try.

- **Racing**. Firm and narrow. Tends to suit lithe, lightweight riders.
- **Mattress**. Springs underneath cushion the bumps.
- **Gel-filled.** The gel squidges itself to the shape of your bottom.
- **Holey.** The gap is meant to provide a little ventilation and ease the pressure on your more delicate bits.
- **Gender-specific.** Saddles designed for the female form tend to be wider and shorter than those made for men.
- **Classic leather.** The high-quality hide gradually softens and conforms to the shape of your nether regions, rather as a pair of handmade shoes fits your feet.
- **Suspension seatpost.** For extra springiness. It telescopes up and down by a few centimetres, ironing out the jolts.

**Handlebars**. Bikes often come with straight bars set low down. These look very sporty, but they force you to adopt a stretched-out riding position which some people find uncomfortable. You might prefer bars of a different shape.

- **Riser bars.** Allow you to ride in a more upright position.
- **Curved bars.** Eases the pressure on your wrists.
- **Dropped bars.** An acquired taste, but the first choice for racers and many long-distance cyclists.
- **Bar ends.** Can be attached to most handlebar types. They enable you to move your hands into slightly different positions as you ride and so avoid numbness.

**Tyres**. The handlebars and the saddle are two points where bike and body converge. The tyres are the point where the whole caboodle meets the road, and they have a crucial effect on the way the bike handles and rides.

- **Knobbly.** Fine for mountains and mud, but on tarmac they provide little grip and take more effort to move.
- **Slick.** A smooth tyre with recessed tread. Provides good grip and an easy ride.
- **Semi-slick.** Meant to give you the best of both worlds. A slick tyre with knobbly bits at the edges for when you ride off road.

**15: Mudguards.** These add a little weight to a bike and fractionally impair its aerodynamic efficiency. And if you routinely ride through thick mud or hurtle through swamps, the gap between guard and wheel can get blocked and the bike will shudder to a halt. These things matter if you're a racing cyclist or a serious mountain biker. However, for the majority of cyclists mudguards are extremely useful: they keep both you and the bike clean. They should really be standard equipment on city bikes, tourers or hybrids. If they're not, get them fitted, and choose mudguards that fasten to the frame with proper metal stays rather than plastic clip-ons, which shake loose all too easily.

**16: Accessorize**. There are a million and one extra bits of kit you can add to your bike. However, bear in mind that anything you add increases the bike's weight – and, if it's a valuable item, you will have to remove it every time you park the bike.

I asked a few friends what accessories they recommended, and was bombarded with ideas including trip computer, map holder, heart-rate monitor, thermos flask (fits in the bike's bottle cage), mobile phone holder, air horn and a sheepskin saddle cover. (These were seven different people,

you understand, not one heavily loaded kleptomaniac.)

Personally, I can't live without a propstand. If I want to stop for a rest the bike stands smartly to attention ready for immediate use. I can oil, load or adjust the bike without it toppling over. Marvellous.

**17: Inflate**. All tyres should be pumped up regularly (see Tip 90). Under-inflated tyres are prone to punctures, give a bumpy ride, and create loads of extra friction which you have to overcome by pedalling harder.

**18: Lighten up**. There are heavy riders and light riders, and the difference has little to do with body mass. Heavy riders keep their bottoms stuck to the saddle, their neck and arms straight and their hands clamped tightly round the handlebars. Ride like this and you feel every bump and imperfection in the road surface. The bike seems to be fighting you and it's an effort to retain control.

It's far better to ride light. If you see a rough bit of road ahead, freewheel. Rise up out of the saddle, lean forward slightly and relax your arms and legs. Keep hold of the bars, but loosely, not in a death grip. The bike will clatter over the bumps but all the shock and vibration will be dispersed.

Some people do this kind of thing instinctively; for others it takes time to develop a technique. If you're new to cycling you may not have sufficient strength in your leg muscles at first, but persevere. Get it right and you'll be able to cycle longer and further and will feel less weary at the end of each ride.

# 3: Clothing

The style-conscious cyclist has a breathtaking range of clothing to choose from. Most of the larger bike shops have a clothing section. Cycling clothes can be expensive, but there are several good reasons for taking the plunge and investing in quality gear. For a start you'll get garments made from advanced materials: outerwear that manages to be simultaneously tough, supple, weatherproof and breathable, and shorts and shirts that wick moisture away from the skin, keeping you dry and comfortable.

Good-quality cycling clothes will also be well designed and can enhance safety. Sleeves, for example, will be a tad longer than those on normal clothes because most people adopt a slightly stretched-forward riding position. Hoods on rain jackets will turn with your head so as not to obstruct your vision. Pockets will be easy to reach. Companies such as Corinne Dennis and Ugogirl recognise that the sexes are proportioned differently, and produce cycling clothes designed specifically for women.

Natty gear abounds, but you won't need a completely new wardrobe to go cycling. You can ride wearing pretty much anything at all (but see Tips 20 and 21). Or, indeed, nothing at all – as the participants in the annual World Naked Bike Ride proudly demonstrate every year (do visit **www.worldnakedbikeride.org**).

**19: Soft and stretchy.** Clothes made from stiff materials with thick seams may be OK for short journeys, but over longer distances they're less comfortable. They rub – and you get sore. Jeans are the worst offenders. Clothes that are designed specifically for cycling are made from soft, stretchy materials. Trousers or leggings will have an extra seam at the knee to allow for the bending and flexing that goes with pedalling. Seams in general will be padded or positioned in such a way as to prevent chafing.

**20: Added padding.** You might appreciate a spot of padding around the palms of your hands to prevent numbness (see Tip 24). And you will certainly benefit from a bit around your hindquarters. Proper cycling shorts have a padded seat and are made from six or eight pieces (or panels) of stretchy, figure-hugging Lycra. Eight-panel shorts tend to fit better. There are shorts specially shaped for men and for women. Lycra cycle shorts are meant to be worn (drop to hushed whisper) without underwear!

A common complaint is that buttocks clad in black Lycra resemble a pair of giant sea slugs. If this bothers you, try using cycling undershorts. These take the place of your normal underwear and are topped off with conventional shorts, trousers or a skirt.

**21: Tie it down.** Your bike is like a whirlpool – anything that gets too close to the wheels or chain will be sucked in. Trousers are particularly at risk, followed closely by those drawstring cords that hang from cagoules and the like. You should secure any loose, flappy items of clothing. Tuck your trousers into your socks or use rubber bands, cycle clips or Velcroed leg bands.

**22: Lotsa layers.** You soon warm up when you're cycling so you need less clothing than you might imagine. That chunky cable-knit sweater might seem essential when you first emerge from the house, but after a few miles I guarantee you'll be taking it off and wondering where to put it.

The best way to control your body temperature is to wear several thin layers and then add or remove items as required. On very cold days keep the soft, porous layers close to your skin and wear something windproof as an outer 'shell'. The nether garments form an insulating layer and the shell keeps the heat in.

**23: B-r-e-a-t-h-e!** You'll stay a lot more comfortable if your outer shell layer is made from a breathable material. This is especially true with rainwear. Without a degree of breathability or ventilation your perspiration condenses and you quickly become hot and bothered, sticky and sore. Gore-Tex is the most famous breathable fabric, but there are several others. If the high-tech approach doesn't appeal, try waxed cotton or simply go for loose-fitting outer garments with openings that aid airflow.

**24**: **Hand in glove.** At night or on cold days your hands can become chilled to the point of pain amazingly quickly. Gloves, of course, are the solution. They need to be thick enough to keep your hands warm, yet thin enough for you to flex your fingers, change gear and brake properly. Gloves lined with Thinsulate material do the job. Wearing gloves in winter and fingerless mitts in summer will also protect your hands from vibration (see Tip 38).

**25**: **Sensible shoes.** I'm told that cycling in high heels is possible but a trifle challenging. Steer clear of sandals too: stubbing a toe at even two miles an hour is no laughing matter. Otherwise, any sort of shoe is fine so long as it allows you to keep your feet on the pedals and to slide them off again when you need to. Pedals fitted with toe clips enable you to put more oomph into pedalling, but if you use them you'll need shoes that can be withdrawn from the toe clips very quickly. It's best to check that out before embarking on a journey.

**26**: **Think about cycle helmets**. In the cycling world there is an ongoing discussion – to put it mildly – on the benefits of cycle helmets and whether people should be encouraged or even compelled to wear them. At present, helmets are optional in the UK.

Advocates of helmets see them as a common-sense safety measure that can reduce head injuries and save lives. The sceptics argue that the amount of protection provided by a cycle helmet is routinely overstated. They fear that compulsory helmet wearing would actually make cycling more dangerous because it would cause levels of cycling to fall and the 'safety in numbers' effect to be lost (see Tip 105).

If you're the sort of person who relishes a vigorous discussion of, say, religion or politics, you'll want to read up and get stuck into the helmet debate (see **www.cyclehelmets.org** and www.bhit.org). If that's not for you,

you should still consider the issue and decide your own personal helmet policy

## Cycle helmets

If you choose to wear a cycle helmet, do three things:

- **Wear it properly**. Buy a helmet that's the right size. Hold the helmet and try turning your head. If your head moves while the helmet stays still, the helmet is too big. The straps should be fastened snugly. The helmet should sit squarely on your head, never worn slung back like a cowboy hat or pulled rakishly forwards.

- **Be consistent.** It's totally illogical to wear a helmet for certain trips but not for others, or to take it off when the weather's warm and have it swinging from your handlebars. If you decide to wear a helmet, wear it for all journeys, however brief. Make it part of your cycling routine.
- **Be realistic.** A helmet does not make you invulnerable: it's not armour plating. Helmets are designed to offer some protection if you fall off your bike and bump your head. (Incidentally, if that does happen, the helmet will need to be replaced. As it will if you drop it on to a hard surface from a height of more than one and a half metres.) Nor will wearing a helmet make you a more competent cyclist. It won't improve your control skills, enhance your judgment, or enable you to influence how other road users treat you. Cycle training, however, can do all of these things (see Chapter 4).

# 4: Learn to ride

Most people are taught to cycle by a family member or friend. Then, beyond a spot of Cycling Proficiency in the school playground, they generally have no further training. But everyone would benefit from some expert instruction, and over recent years there has been a mushrooming of schemes offering adult cycle training.

For beginners there's off-road training to instil basic skills and to build confidence. For more advanced riders there's on-road training, learning to handle a wide variety of traffic conditions. Your instructor will show you how seemingly simple things, such as where on the road you ride, can have a significant influence on the way other road users perceive and treat you.

Before their training many people are somewhat sceptical. But afterwards they're exuberant! The whole experience of riding in traffic suddenly feels so much easier. 'I learned things I didn't know I didn't know,' was how one satisfied trainee summed it up.

The tips in this chapter come from professional cycling instructors. If they whet your appetite for improving your cycling skills, book yourself a lesson. There's a national helpline to help you find out who provides adult cycle training in your area: phone **0870 607 0415**.

**27: Study traffic**. It may sound as exciting as proofreading telephone directories, but it can be remarkably instructive to stand by a busy road junction and watch what goes on. Why has that car stopped there? When will it move off again? Why is that car signalling? What manoeuvre is the driver planning to make? When that lorry turns left, how much room will it need? What's that bus going to do? And so on.

You'll discover that, far from being the free-for-all it's sometimes depicted as, 'traffic' is a predictable system, governed by rules and conventions. Sometimes these are bent or broken, but it's usually possible to anticipate where and when this will happen.

Pay particular attention to any cyclists who use the junction you're observing. Do they ride in a predictable way? Do they make it easy for other road users to understand what it is they want to do? Would you have ridden the junction like that? If not, what would you have done differently? Analyse other people's errors and their successes, and learn from them.

**28: Use the road (1).** Some cyclists, for perfectly understandable reasons, think that they'll be safest riding on the pavement. In fact, that's a myth. Drivers pulling out of, or going into, side turnings will not see you. Nor will people stepping out of shop doorways. On top of that, most pedestrians find bikes on pavements annoying or intimidating. Importantly, riding on the pavement is against the law and you could be given an on-the-spot fine.

**29: Use the road (2).** The gutter is no better than pavement. Don't go there. In law, you're entitled to use all of the road, so long as you don't needlessly impede others.

On busy urban roads where there are parked cars and other obstructions, this means taking up the primary riding position – the centre of the traffic lane. Riding there puts you clear of parked vehicles and of car doors being flung open, and it means that you're in the attention zone of other road users. They can see you and you have a good line of sight yourself. At first, it takes a certain steely determination to ride like this – it can feel as though you're putting yourself in danger or causing a nuisance. But actually you're riding safely, predictably and lawfully as part of the traffic flow.

When the traffic is moving more rapidly and there is sufficient road space, you should take up the secondary riding position – to the left of the traffic lane, about 30 inches or 80 centimetres out from the kerb.

Understanding these two concepts – primary and secondary riding – and learning how to move seamlessly between them is an essential skill. Go practise!

**30: Think outside the box.** Cycle lanes, advanced stop lines, cyclist contraflows, toucan crossings, elephants' footprints*... Across the land, highway engineers have been busy tinkering with our roads and adding facilities that are intended to benefit cyclists. Sometimes these additions are helpful; sometimes not. A common complaint about cycle lanes, for example, is that they stop just at the point where they're most needed. But cycle lanes are intended for guidance only. They're not strips of magic carpet, guaranteed to give cyclists an easy ride. Nor do they set the boundaries of where you can cycle. The road is yours to use in its entirety. Cycle where it's easiest and safest.

*Square-shaped blobs of paint marked on the road to delineate a cycle crossing.*

**31: Look behind.** Learner drivers are taught 'mirror... signal... manoeuvre'. The look in the mirror tells them whether there are vehicles behind, and how fast they're approaching. You can buy rear-view mirrors for bicycles, but they give you a very limited field of vision, they're quickly shaken out of alignment, and they get pinched. It's far easier to just take a look.

If you try simply rotating your head on its axis, like an owl, you'll only manage a quarter turn and you'll probably get neck strain. Instead, try bending your arms at the elbows and leaning forwards slightly, towards the handlebars. Push your chin towards your shoulder, lower your shoulder a little, and then turn your head and upper body. You should get a good rearward view.

An alternative technique involves holding the bars with one hand and keeping that arm straight. Lower your other arm to your side (ready to give a signal), straighten up and then twist your head and upper body to the rear, looking over the shoulder of the arm you've lowered.

Both methods sounds like fiendish pieces of contortion but, with practice, you'll be able to look behind swiftly and smoothly and without wobbling.

**32:** **Ask yourself questions**. As you ride, ask yourself the following questions. Where am I going? How am I going to get there? What am I going to do? What do I need to think about? It's a similar exercise to standing at the roadside watching traffic (see Tip 27). This time, though, you're part of the traffic and the process is a lot more rapid.

## Try this exercise

In your mind, as you ride along, break your journey down into short stretches of about 250 metres. Think about each stage and ask yourself these questions.

- **Where am I going?** 'I'm cycling along West Street and I want to turn right, into Hill Road...'
- **How am I going to get there?** 'By changing my riding position, and doing a right turn, just past that phone box...'
- **What am I going to do?** 'I'm going to look behind, move from the secondary riding position into the primary position so as to be clear of those parked cars. I'm going to look behind again, signal right and, if it's clear, move towards the centre of the road but still to the left of the white line...'
- **What do I need to think about?** 'I'll need to slow down as I draw level with the turning. I'll need to change into a lower gear. I'm looking for a gap in the oncoming traffic. If there isn't one I'll need to stop and wait and be ready to move off again...'

- **Now where am I going?** 'Up Hill Road, through those roadworks and then left at the traffic lights by the Texaco garage...'
And so on...

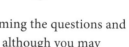

Analysing your journey in this way and actually forming the questions and the answers in your mind (or out loud if you prefer, although you may attract a few stares) is empowering. It makes you really understand what you're doing and why you're doing it.

**33:** ACE signalling. It's easy to give a signal in a car – you just flick the indicator arm. Signalling on a bike is a weightier matter. It involves sticking your arm out, an action which reduces your control of the steering and your ability to brake by 50 per cent. So don't signal unnecessarily – do it only when another road user needs to know what you're up to, and sustain the signal for just enough time to get your message across.

In short, a signal should be ACE: Appropriate to the conditions, Clear to other road users, and Effective in getting you where you want to go.

**34**: **Eye contact.** When you're cycling in traffic you need to be certain that drivers have truly seen you and understood that you need a bit of time and road space to complete your manoeuvre. If possible, try to establish eye contact with them. Drivers then recognise you as a human being rather than as a mere object. If their attention was drifting, it gets refocused.

**35**: **Courtesy.** In all the turmoil of an urban rush hour it's easy to forget that traffic is just people (albeit people in charge of a couple of tons of metal). Lots of them, all trying to get somewhere.

Occasionally, when other road uses are impolite or do stupid things, it's tempting to gesticulate or lash out in some way. My advice is to refrain. Let it go. Your hands should be on the bars, controlling your bike. Your eyes and your mind should be fixed on the road ahead. Getting angry is distracting and wastes energy.

However, if a fellow road user does you a favour – maybe slows down to let you join a queue of traffic, or drops back on a narrow stretch of road and waits to overtake when they can give you a wide berth – then signal your approval. Raise a hand in thanks, or at the very least raise a smile. Such small courtesies oil the social wheels and make drivers more inclined to be nice to cyclists in future.

# 5: Body

If we're to stay healthy we need to exercise. Anything is better than nothing, but cycling comes close to being the ideal activity. If you ride a bike you don't need to join a club or haul yourself along to a gym or fitness centre, nor do you need any specialised equipment apart from the bike itself. You don't have to take time out for cycling – simply convert some of your routine car or public transport trips to pedal power and there's your exercise for the day.

Riding a bike exercises most of the major muscles and it increases lung capacity. It improves the functioning of the heart and blood vessels, decreasing your risk of coronary disease. Cycling will reduce the likelihood of your developing diabetes, it can help stabilise or lower your blood pressure, and it can even protect against several sorts of cancer. Cycling does all this while burning about 300 calories an hour – so it can help with weight control too.

Adults who cycle regularly are reckoned to have a fitness level equivalent to being 10 years younger! Ride a bike and you'll feel and look better – and you may well live longer.

## 36: Drink water.

Up to 75 per cent of your lovely body is made up of water. Precious though it is, however, we keep losing the stuff. Some disappears every time we go to the loo, and we also emit water as vapour on our breath and through the pores of our skin. When you cycle the combination of raised metabolism and airflow means you can dehydrate rapidly and often without realising. You rarely feel hot and sweaty on a bike.

The consequences of dehydration can range from tiredness, dizziness and headaches through to heat exhaustion or even full-blown heatstroke. Dehydration is more of a hazard during hot weather, but you dry out in the depths of winter too.

The solution is simple: drink water. Get into the habit of carrying water with you. Fit a bottle cage to your bike so you can keep a supply to hand. Tap water is fine, as is bottled water (the body prefers still to fizzy) or fruit squash. The sportier bike magazines are packed with ads for isotonic energy drinks, and they're OK if you can afford them. But be sceptical about their supposed benefits – you don't need all those salts and minerals unless you're really pushing yourself.

**37**: **Use sunscreen.** When you're cycling there's a constant flow of cool air over your body, and this can keep you cheerfully unaware of the fact that you're getting sunburnt. The back of the neck is particularly at risk. It's wise to carry sunscreen and to make regular use of it.

**38**: **Protect your palms**. The ulnar nerve that runs from your hand up the length of your arm is sensitive to vibration, especially if you hold your hand in a single position for long periods. Inflammation of the nerve – called ulnar neuropathy or, rather more quaintly, handlebar palsy – can occur surprisingly quickly, especially if you ride over rough terrain. Symptoms range from pins-and-needles through to numbness or, in extreme cases, pain and paralysis.

Avoid it by providing some cushioning. Cycling gloves, or fingerless mitts with gel padding are cheap and very effective, as are gel- or foam-filled handlebar grips. Suspension forks or a suspension handlebar stem cost a lot more and need to be professionally fitted, but will noticeably reduce the amount of road shock to your hands.

You should also periodically try to change the way you grip the bars. Straight handlebars allow only one position. Fit bar ends (See Tip 14) and you've got at least two ways of holding on. Other designs of handlebar give you a choice of several positions and are recommended if you regularly ride longer distances.

**39:** **Nurse those knees.** If your knees hurt after riding your bike then something is awry and you need to look into it, or you run the risk of long-term injury. Check your saddle height. If it's set too low your knees are twisting outwards and that's bad. Too high and you're stretching your knee joints, which is equally wrong. See Tip 13 for setting your saddle properly.

Think about how you pedal too. If you habitually select high gears and push the pedals quite forcefully you're stressing your knee joints. The human body likes lots of light, repetitive movements rather than fewer, more powerful ones. So choose a slightly lower gear. You'll turn the cranks more rapidly but it will take less effort and it won't strain your knees.

**40:** **Bottom!** Some people seem able to hop on to a bike – any bike – and ride long distances in total comfort. Others find that even short rides leave them wincing and walking like John Wayne after crossing the High Sierras. But take heart: saddle soreness can be prevented! Take the time to find a saddle that's right for you (see Tip 14) and set it at the correct height (Tip 13). Wear shorts or leggings (Tip 20) that are designed for cycling and are padded in the appropriate places.

You need to give a new saddle time to break in, and you need to allow your derriere time to adapt to the experience of perching upon it. Start with short rides, a couple of times each week if possible – rides that finish well before anything starts hurting. You should find that you can gradually cycle further and further with no sign of soreness.

**41:** **Eat.** Many a bike ride has begun with a full English breakfast, paused for a picnic at lunchtime, refuelled on scones, jam and clotted cream mid-afternoon, and concluded with a three-course dinner – and hooray for that! Cycling gives you a healthy appetite and the casual cyclist can feel free to indulge.

The flipside of having a good appetite is that it quickly turns into raging hunger, so your ride should take in a few pit stops. Never rely on isolated village pubs to come up with the goods. If you do, some perverse cosmic law ensures that when you, your family and friends and a gaggle of small starving children arrive at the Cat and Ferret you'll discover that the restaurant is closed, the chef is off sick or that the pub was converted into timeshare apartments five years ago.

So carry some tucker with you. Chocolate melts, boiled sweets have no nutritional value, and crisps and salted peanuts make you thirsty. The best cycle snacks are dried fruit, seeds and (unsalted) nuts. They don't take up much room and they won't come to harm at the bottom of your bag.

**42: Eat – sensibly.** If you're cycling more than your customary distance, or you're embarking on a cycling holiday, you might want to plan your meals with more care. The body performs best on a diet that has a little less fat and protein, and rather more carbohydrate – especially the unrefined forms such as brown rice, wholemeal bread and pasta – than you might usually consume. These foods release their energy gradually, meaning that you feel satisfied for longer and are less inclined to hunger pangs.

**43: Watch your eyes**. Sunglasses will protect your eyes against glare, and they also guard against the peril of flying insects. When you're zooming down a hill at 50 kilometers an hour, about to negotiate a bend, a gnat under the eyelid is truly unsettling. As well as designer shades, bike shops sell protective glasses with clear lenses for use on duller days.

# 6: Pootling

You're pootling when you pedal off, in an optimistic frame of mind, for a gentle ride that can last for anything from an hour to a full day. Piece several pootles together and you have a cycling holiday. Pootlers choose routes on the basis of their beauty, the places of interest they pass through and the refreshment opportunities en route. They prefer quiet country lanes to busy A-roads, and they value comfort over speed. Pootlers are usually up for an unexpected detour to a place with an interesting name, or an extended lunch break.

Opportunities for pootling are plentiful. There are thousands of idyllic miles of road and lane and bridleway to be enjoyed – and more routes are being created all the time. With a little research you can pick up lightly trafficked routes and specially made cycle tracks that rapidly leave the madding crowds behind.

This chapter is about how to discover the best cycling country, either by doing some groundwork yourself, or (because many pootlers have a slightly lazy streak) by tagging on to someone else's ride and getting all the planning done for you.

**44: Map read.** I once cycled from Bristol to Oxford, planning my route on the day I set off. Almost the entire journey was on quiet lanes, weaving through sleepy villages and pastoral landscapes that hadn't changed much in centuries.

The key to discovering this rural tranquillity was to use a map. Every good bookstore and outdoor shop sells Ordnance Survey maps. The Landranger series (pink cover) has a scale of 1:50,000 (two centimetres to the kilometre), while the Explorer series (orange cover) has a more detailed 1:25,000 scale (four centimetres to the kilometre). Both series cover the whole of the UK. The quiet lanes sought after by cyclists are the C-class roads, coloured in yellow.

If you prefer someone else to blaze a trail for you, check out the maps published by Goldeneye (see **www.goldeneyemaps.com**). These show a selection of circular bike rides in some of the most picturesque places. You can also get ideas for rides from books, bike magazines and Sunday newspapers. The rides are usually graded according to how long and how strenuous they are, and often include good advice about where to eat and park.

**45: Maps for free.** Many local councils produce cycle maps of their area. If there's a charge it's normally only a pound or two, but as a rule they're free. Increasingly, council websites have a page or two devoted to cycling, with maps available as downloads.

Some maps are better than others. The worst are cluttered up with useless information such as routes that are planned but haven't yet been built. The best are designed in collaboration with local cyclists and show recommended on-road routes, quiet backstreets, useful shortcuts, cycle tracks and bike shops. They're helpful for navigating about town, but also for getting out of town and into the country.

**46: Follow the signs.** Most areas have officially sanctioned cycle trails. These are circular or linear routes designed to take in attractive scenery and interesting places. Free maps are usually available from the local council (see Tip 45) and, to make them even easier to follow, the routes are signposted.

In addition to local routes, there is a National Cycle Network in the UK. Planned by the charity Sustrans and part-funded by millions of pounds of National Lottery money, it now totals 10,000 miles. Sustrans claims that half the UK population lives within one mile of its routes. Almost a third of the network is traffic free, using railway paths, riversides or forest trails, while the rest is on-road. It's intended to be family friendly: hundreds of cycle lanes, signal-controlled crossings and bridges have been built so that you rarely have to mix with heavy traffic.

The routes have alluring names such as the Cuckoo Trail, the Centurion Way and the Sea to Sea (or C2C for short). They are all numbered and waymarked: look for the little red, white and blue road signs.

**47: Go organised.** Once a year, the busy A4 trunk road along the Avon Gorge into central Bristol is closed to cars and turned over to cyclists. Instead of the usual fumes and the grinding of engines, there's fresh air, birdsong and the swish of bicycle wheels. The event, called Bristol's Biggest Bike Ride, attracts around 4,000 people of all ages and abilities. Similar rides take place in other parts of the country. Nottingham, for example, has the Great Nottinghamshire Bike Ride, and many large charities organise fundraising rides.

You normally have to register to join an organised ride. If it's in aid of a particular charity you'll be expected to raise sponsorship money. Make sure you understand the distances you'll be undertaking and ensure that your bike is in good condition. Apart from that, you can pretty much leave things to the organisers. Big rides often have marshals positioned at key points to help you along, plus mechanics and First Aiders in case of mishaps.

Organised rides let you see places from a fresh perspective, and there's something exhilarating about riding with others (in the case of the London-to-Brighton Bike Ride, up to 27,000 others – a great two-wheeled tide!)

**48: Ride with a guide.** For the ultimate in relaxed biking you can book a day ride or an entire family holiday with one of many cycle tour companies. They will plan the routes that you'll ride, sort out your accommodation, lay on scrumptious food and carry your luggage. All you have to do is pedal and enjoy the scenery. One holiday company (sadly, no longer trading) used to have a band of mediaeval minstrels on its payroll. They would join the riders towards the end of each day's trip to spur them on them with a few rousing tunes.

Closer to home, you're likely to find a club or a local cycle campaign running rides at weekends. Newcomers are usually welcome, although if you make a habit of riding with a particular group you should pay your dues and become a member. You won't be pampered in the same way as on a cycling holiday (don't expect minstrels) but you'll get to ride a planned and researched route. Before joining a club ride, it's wise to contact the organiser and find out whether the distances they cover and the pace at which they ride are within your capabilities.

**49**: **Get up early**. At half-past four on a Sunday morning even our most congested towns and cities are magically free of traffic. True, it takes a bit of willpower to wrench yourself out of bed at such an hour, even in summer – but it's worth it. A spin round a big city at first light is an experience you'll remember forever. The air is fresh, the buildings glisten in the pale sunlight, the hush is almost palpable… There are sights and smells that you just don't get during the rest of the day. If you're an early bird, the world's your oyster – at least for a couple of hours.

# 7: To work!

Why limit your cycling to leisure rides at weekends and on holiday? Bikes are practical machines, easily able to handle serious commuting. Cycle to work and you'll save money on petrol, parking and other running costs. If you're able to forgo your car (or second car) completely, you'll save an absolute fortune and be able to pay off your mortgage and go on a world cruise every year.

Commuting by bike will keep you fit, save you the cost of gym membership, and help you manage the stresses of the working day. As well as radiating good health you'll be entitled to a glow of pride for having done your bit for the environment. Cycling reduces your carbon footprint from bovver boot to ballet shoe.

While the pootler (see Chapter 6) thrives on spontaneity and relishes the unexpected, the cycle commuter needs to be more organised. Equipment has to be reliable and procedures rock solid. This chapter will help you to plan and prepare. The first few times you ride to work it might feel slightly strange. But stick with it for a month, get the details right, and you'll never go back to your old method.

**50**: **Check out your workplace.** Some employers welcome cyclists with open arms and state-of-the-art bike parking, lockers, changing rooms and showers. Others are less accommodating. If you're planning to commute by bike you need to inspect your workplace and see how it shapes up.

If your journey isn't too challenging you might only need somewhere to park your bike. If there are no cycle racks, find a suitable solid object and lock up to that (see Tip 74). But if your commute leaves you in a muck sweat (although this might be avoidable, see Tip 55), you'll have to freshen up in the loo if there are no showers. You're likely to have a pannier or rucksack with you, waterproofs on damp days, and possibly lights and a cycle helmet. Think about where they can be stored.

If your organisation already has a number of cyclists it's more likely to provide decent facilities. Oddly enough, there are also benefits in being the only person who cycles. Play your cards right and management may come to regard you as a loveable eccentric and allow you special privileges such as taking your bike into the building or showering in the executive washroom.

**51**: **Plan your route.** Even in the most congested cities there are usually quiet back streets and lightly trafficked roads that are great for cycling. You can also exploit routes that aren't available to motorists: cycle tracks, canal towpaths and often shortcuts through parks and other open spaces.

Study street plans and, if your area has one, the relevant cycle map (see Tips 45 and 46). You can also search online using the excellent Google maps. Click the 'terrain' button to get a map combined with an aerial photograph to get a feel for the landscape.

**52**: **Rehearse.** Having identified a few possible routes, take time at the weekend or on an evening to ride them. Things will look and feel very different on the ground. When you've found a route you like, ride it from home to work and then back again. Make a note of how long it takes. Come Monday morning when you ride it for real, allow that amount of time plus around thirty per cent to take account of busier conditions and unexpected delays.

**53**: **Push.** If your planned route is 90 per cent perfect but still has bits you find disconcerting (and they can't be avoided), don't be afraid to get off and wheel your bike. It's not being wimpish or breaking any kind of rule. The wise cyclist always rides within, never beyond, their abilities. As you get accustomed to cycle commuting and your skill and confidence improve, solutions may occur to you. Or you may pick up a few tricks from watching others. If adult cycle training (see Chapter 4) is available in your area, book some expert instruction on how to handle the more challenging sections of your route.

**54**: **Get your boss to pay**. The Government-backed Cycle to Work scheme gives employers generous tax breaks that allow them to purchase bikes and sell them on to their staff, deducting a small amount from the employee's pay packet each month. Savings depend on the nature of the

business and the employee's tax band, but it's possible to get a bike plus accessories such as a lock, lights and panniers for half the manufacturers' list price. See if your employer runs such a scheme – or, if they don't, suggest that they do.

**55**: **Change at work.** In Ostend once I was captivated by the sight of both male and female customs officers biking to work on big sit-up-and-beg roadsters, gliding off for a light lunch at noon, and then cycling home in the evening. All in full uniform, gold braid gleaming; not a speck of dirt on them or a hair out of place.

So it's certainly possible to cycle to work wearing a suit. But many people find it easier to wear cycling gear for the journey and then change into more formal gear on arrival. If you have to carry your work clothes with you they'll keep their shape better if you roll them round a towel, rather than folding them. There are also special garment bags that attach to your bike. If things are still a bit crumpled you could give them a once-over with a travel iron.

Another option is to drive to work on a Monday with a week's supply of clothing, and then cycle in on the other four days. Of course, you'll need somewhere to store everything – ideally in a cabinet or locker tall enough to hang the garments.

**56**: **No sweat**. Cars have had air-conditioning only relatively recently; bikes, on the other hand, have had it for years. As you ride, the air rushing past keeps you cool, even if you're riding with gusto. But problems arise when you come to a halt – and they quadruple once you step indoors. Suddenly you have the complexion of a boiled lobster; your pores open and you start perspiring.

Avoid the problem by taking it easy for the last half mile or so. Ride at about two thirds of your usual speed and freewheel whenever possible. Athletic types may need to force themselves to take it slow. If you're wearing a jacket, open it up and let the breeze wash over you. You'll also stay cooler if you carry stuff on the bike, rather than on your back (see Tip 64).

# 8 : Baby on board

Children like cycling. As babies they're fascinated by the sensation of movement, and from the vantage point of a child seat or the security of a cycle trailer they get to see, hear and wave to the outside world. Once they start cycling themselves a bike means freedom and fun.

If adults need a minimum of 30 minutes' exercise every day, children should have at least twice that amount, but vast numbers of kids get nothing like enough. About 15 per cent of children in the UK are overweight or obese, and the problem, like the children, is increasing. As we saw in Chapter 5, cycling is excellent exercise. Get into it as a kid and the chances are that it will become a lifelong habit.

There's equipment galore to keep you and your brood on two wheels. This chapter is about carrying young children by bike, from your child's first few months right through to the time when they get a bike of their own.

**57: Fit a child seat.** Once your child can sit up unaided and hold their head up unaided, usually from the age of six months or so, they're ready to go cycling. Fit your bike with a good-quality child seat and you're away. Most children love the experience and respond with gurgles of satisfaction.

Front-mounted seats allow you to keep an eye on your passenger and to talk to them. However, you might find steering the bike difficult with a baby up front, in which case go for a rear-mounted seat.

Seats that are rated BS EN 14344 are approved to carry children weighing 9–22 kg. Buy your seat from a reputable bike shop and expect to pay at least £30. Pay more and you'll get a seat that reclines (useful for very young children when they want to sleep) and comes with features such as an adjustable headrest, a rain cover and storage compartments. All seats should have a safety harness and foot guards to keep tiny toes away from the bike's wheels. More information is available on the RoSPA website: **www.rospa.com/RoadSafety/advice/cycling/carrying_children.htm.**

**58: Tow a trailer.** With a trailer, you and your offspring can cycle further and take all the paraphernalia of childhood along with you. Kids love trailers. They can play with their toys, eat and drink, shout and sing, and eventually fall asleep. The child sits on a comfortable hammock-type seat, strapped in with a safety harness and protected further by the trailer's roll-cage. They can enjoy the fresh air on fine days, or be safely tucked away behind wind- and waterproof panels during bad weather. Upmarket trailers convert into stylish baby buggies, which can be very handy when you reach your destination.

Trailers are more expensive than child seats and you have to get used to the extra weight and width when riding. They were once quite an unusual sight, but now many companies are making them. Burley and Chariot are two manufacturers with a lot of experience and a good reputation. There are trailers for a single child and some that will take two.

**59: Tag-a-long.** Also known as trailer bikes, these are child-size bicycles with a tow bar instead of a front wheel. A hinged attachment links it to your seatpost and the two of you ride in tandem. You remain in full control of the steering and braking, but both riders pedal – or the rear rider freewheels if they are getting tired. Upmarket tag-a-longs have gears so that the youngster can vary their pedalling cadence.

Tag-a-longs allow families to cycle safely in town as well as in open country. Children feel very involved and grown up, and adults can relax knowing that junior isn't riding erratically or pedalling off in the wrong direction.

Children are ready for a tag-a-long at about four years old. As they grow,

the height of the saddle and the handlebars can be raised. When the tag-a-long is no longer needed, sell it – they command good prices second-hand.

**60: Be wary of stabilisers.** They sound like a good idea: two arms either side of the bike with little wheels attached to help keep the young rider upright. Junior can learn to pedal and to steer without the risk of taking a tumble. However, there are two problems with this approach. Firstly, bikes are not inherently upright machines. Riding them is a process of learning to balance by making thousands of minor corrections as you go along. The process should become automatic and intuitive, stabilisers can make that process longer than it need be.

The other drawback of stabilisers is that they're effective only some of the time. If the child lurches particularly sharply to one side, the stabiliser will act as a pivot and flip the bike over in spectacular fashion. I've seen it happen a number of times. True, the kids always survived, but it can't have been a happy experience.

**61: Get a hobby.** There is a gentler way to introduce children to the rudiments of cycling. It involves using a modern-day interpretation of the hobbyhorse. One such device is the Like-a-Bike – a stylish thing made from blonde plywood. The Like-a-Bike has two wheels, handlebars, and a seat, but no pedals or chain. The child sits on it and moves forward by scooting. Kids love the sensation of gliding along under their own power and, without any coaxing, soon learn to lift their feet up so as to get the most from each scoot. They're balancing on two wheels. Any problems and they can put both feet to the floor instantly.

Children as young as two will enjoy playing with a hobbyhorse. When they've fully mastered it, it's time to present them with their first proper bicycle. But do two things: lower the saddle so they can put both feet flat on the floor, and unscrew the pedals. Let them scoot along. Once they're scooting with confidence and have mastered the basics of steering and braking, refit the pedals – and watch them cycle!

**62: Buy quality.** A typical child's bike can often weigh almost as much as an adult-sized tourer and be made of cheap, irreparable components. On top of that, many parents insist on buying their youngster a bike that is several sizes too large, on the assumption that they will grow into it.

Despite having such dismal equipment inflicted on them, most kids take to cycling with great zeal. But how much better it would be if they had a decent a bike that fitted them properly! They'd be safer. They'd begin to understand how things like gears work, and they could help with maintenance.

High-quality children's bicycles take some tracking down (try Islabikes and the unfortunately named Puky), and you'll pay at least twice what you would for a bike from a supermarket or toy shop. But the good bikes are veritable jewels: lightweight and well equipped; specially proportioned to fit small riders and to give them a taste of real cycling.

**63: Get Bikeability.** I'd wager that every parent in the land has heard of Cycling Proficiency. As a 'brand' it's been a rip-roaring success, but as a guarantee of quality, it's always been variable. Some Cycling Proficiency schemes were excellent courses that showed children how to cycle skilfully on today's roads. Others did little more than get the kids to ride round the school playground. Happily Cycling Proficiency is now being superseded by a new sort of training called Bikeability. The instructors are experienced cyclists and the courses have to meet a consistent standard. Bikeability aims to equip young people with the knowledge, skills and confidence to carry out proper journeys.

Bikeability training has three levels:

- **Level One** is a beginners' course that teaches children how to control their bikes properly and to carry out basic manoeuvres. It takes place off-road, away from traffic.
  - **Level Two** introduces children to riding on the road. They learn how to start and stop, pull out of junctions, turn left and right and pass parked cars.
  - **Level Three** is the advanced course. It teaches young cyclists how to use roundabouts and multi-lane roads, and how to negotiate complex junctions.

Find out whether your local council's road safety team offers Bikeability training. Check too whether there are any independent training providers in your area. These small, community-minded organisations are passionate about cycling and they employ dedicated people with a vast knowledge and expertise. Their Bikeability training courses can be truly inspiring.

# 9: Loads easier

Sooner or later every cyclist will want to carry a sizeable load. It starts off innocently enough – a few sweets in your pockets, a newspaper stuffed down the back of your trousers, a pullover draped casually over your shoulders… Then, before you know it, you've got two carrier-bagfuls of shopping swinging from your handlebars. This is when things get difficult. The bags act as pendulums, constantly tugging your steering out of line and banging your shopping against the wheels, where the spokes nibble away at it. If you make it home you'll find that your lettuce has been shredded, your salami sliced and your eggs scrambled.

Everyday forms of luggage such as shopping bags, handbags and briefcases – even rucksacks and shoulder bags – aren't particularly easy to use on a bike. It's much better to use equipment designed for the bike. And there are loads to choose from.

Properly equipped, your bike is a veritable workhorse, capable of carrying up to ten times its own weight. People have moved house by bike! You're unlikely to want to do that, but, with the proper gear, you can transport all your bits and pieces easily and with very little extra effort.

**64**: **Let the bike do the work.** Attach your stuff to your bike, rather than to your body. You will stay cool and comfortable, you'll escape backache, and you'll be able to control your bike more precisely.

**65**: **Bag it.** There are several sorts of luggage that fasten straight to the bike.

## Bike luggage

- **Saddle wedges**. These slide on to the rails underneath your saddle. They're just large enough for a little toolkit and maybe a thin, tightly folded rain jacket.
- **Handlebar bags**. Close to hand and always within your sight, these are ideal for storing credit cards, cameras and other valuables. Most have the option of fixing a map holder to the lid of the bag.
- **Saddlebags**. Not very fashionable now, but they have considerable load-carrying capacity. Carradice (**www.carradice.co.uk**) still makes them. The largest models can hold up to 24 litres, which is enough for a small tent and quite a lot of camping gear. They can be fastened directly to your saddle, but only if it has special loops – and most modern saddles don't. Instead, you can buy a mounting that fits to the seatpost, then the bag clips to the mounting.
- **Basket**. An old-fashioned but supremely simple way of transporting stuff. Choose from contemporary wire mesh or traditional, locally sourced, ethically traded, biodegradable willow.

**66**: **Fit a rack.** Many bikes intended for city use or for touring come with a luggage rack (or 'rear carrier') as standard. If your bike hasn't got one they can almost always be added. For bikes with rear suspension there are racks (suitable for light loads only) that clamp on to your seatpost.

Some racks have a spring-loaded gadget that will grip a rolled-up newspaper or a carefully folded jacket. However, the best way to fasten things to a rack is to use bungees – lengths of thick elastic with hooks either end. Bike shops sell them. With a bit of cunning and several bungees you can lash almost anything to your rack – I've seen someone move a folding picnic table and two deckchairs this way.

**67**: **Use panniers.** Panniers are bags specially designed to fit a bicycle. Rear panniers hang either side of your luggage rack. Front ones, which are only really suitable for small, light loads, fasten to special racks on your front fork. Panniers distribute the load evenly and carry it close to the ground (rather than up high as with a rucksack), giving your bike a lower centre of gravity and making it more stable. A single pannier is usually enough for commuting and short leisure rides. A big load will require a pair.

Panniers come in various sizes – the largest are able to swallow an impressive 50 litres' worth of luggage per pannier. Some designs are just a simple bag; others have useful side pockets for storing smaller items. The better panniers have ingenious fastening mechanisms that let you attach them and unclip them in seconds, but which won't shake loose accidentally.

**68**: **Try a trailer**. Add a trailer and your bike becomes a serious load-lugger – capable of moving, if not mountains, then certainly generous hillocks.

Two-wheel trailers have either a platform, a box or a bag for your cargo. One of the most popular and well-thought-out is the Bike-Hod, one version of which is designed to double as a supermarket trolley. You unhitch it from the bike and wheel it round the store, self-scanning items as you go. Pay at the checkout, re-attach the Hod to your bike, and away you go.

Single-wheeled trailers, such as the Bob Yak, can't carry big loads the way a hunky two-wheeled trailer can, and they need to be propped upright while you load them. Their big advantage, however, is that the load sits low down, making everything more stable. They're easier to tow, too: wherever the bike goes, the trailer snakes along behind. You hardly know it's there.

**69**: **Ride light.** With bags attached to your handlebars and saddle, panniers front and rear, and a trailer following behind, your bike is a veritable juggernaut. But just because you can haul a lot of stuff doesn't mean that you should. On a bike, every gramme of weight requires a touch more effort from you, the rider.

Globetrotting cyclists carry small amounts of washing powder rather than several sets of spare clothing. And there are tales told of the cycle tourist who drilled holes in the handles of his toothbrush and all his cutlery; or the chap who, after reading each page of his paperback, tore it out and consigned it to the campfire, just to save weight.

You don't need to go to such extremes, but a bit of preparation before you start will save a lot of effort later.

# 10: Security

Bike theft is epidemic. According to the Home Office, around 150,000 bikes are reported stolen every year and the majority are never recovered. The Transport Research Laboratory reckons that the problem may be far worse – up to 700,000 thefts per year – because so many incidents go unreported. That's a truly staggering one bike every 45 seconds being pinched. All cycles are potential targets, but BMX and mountain bikes are about twice as likely to be stolen than other types.

At a hospital near to where I live, a father and son cruised the grounds every few days in a big white van equipped with massive bolt croppers and other cutting tools. They sliced through locks or through entire bike stands and harvested hundreds of bikes over several years before being caught. If a professional thief takes a shine to your bike it's virtually impossible to stop him.

Happily, most bike theft is not done by professionals: it's opportunistic, and it can be prevented by taking a few simple precautions. This chapter explains how to deter the thief and keep your bike.

**70: The 10-per-cent principle.** Good-quality bike locks don't come cheap. Then again, neither do new bikes. A quality lock is an investment well worth making. Confronted by something challenging, most bike thieves will move on and look for easier pickings elsewhere.

Be prepared to spend about 10 per cent of the cost of your bike on a lock. £250 bike? Get a £25 lock. Those with a 'Sold Secure' logo on the packaging have been through an accreditation process that includes trying to force, cut and pick the lock. They are awarded a bronze, silver or gold accolade according to how well they withstand the assault. Go for gold if you can possibly afford it.

**71**: **D-lock.** The classic bike lock is D-shaped. The best ones have sophisticated mechanisms and are made from specially hardened steel. Open the lock and it splits into two pieces. The curved bar goes through the bike's frame,

through one of the wheels and then around an immovable object such as a bike stand (see Tip 73). You then fit the two bits together and lock it. It takes just a few seconds and quickly becomes second nature.

For extra security you can thread a length of cable with loops either end through the bike's other wheel, through the rails under your saddle, and through anything else that might be stolen, and secure the loops with the bar of the D-lock.

**72**: **Two locks.** Two bike locks offer twice the protection, but quality locks are hefty items and it's not a good idea to lug all that extra weight around. Instead, if you make a regular journey by bike, leave lock number two at your destination. Fasten it to your favourite cycle stand and it'll be there waiting for you.

**73**: **Lock solid.** In some places you'll come across the type of bike parking that the cycling fraternity call wheelbenders – because that's one of their defects. Another defect of these is that, because they only hold the front wheel, a thief simply needs to flick the wheel's quick-release fastening (see Tip 74) to make off with the rest of the bike. Avoid this type of stand if you possibly can and, if you're a campaigning sort of person, lobby for their removal.

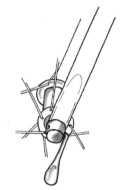

Sheffield stands are much better. If there are no proper stands, lock your bike to something solid and immovable. One caveat, however: if you use a road sign make sure that someone can't just lift the bike and its lock over the top of the sign.

Finally, be wary of locking your bike to railings. Technically, railings are private property and the owners can get extremely shirty. They can't legally impound your bike or damage it. But that won't necessarily stop them.

**74: Remove.** Always remove items such as luggage and lights and carry them with you. And ask your favourite bike shop to remove the quick-release fastenings that you may find on one or both wheels and at the bottom of your seatpost. (If your bike doesn't have them, don't worry).

As the name suggests, quick releases undo in seconds: you just flip the lever and whatever they are fastening can be removed. They can be very useful, enabling you to take off a wheel if you get a puncture, or adjust the height of your saddle speedily and without special tools. Unfortunately, however, thieves find their speed of operation irresistible, and many a bike has been robbed of its saddle or wheels while the owner's back was turned.

**75: Disguise**. One way of reducing a bike's thief appeal is to use gaffer tape to cover the manufacturer's logo and any other decals or badges. Many thieves are brand conscious and will overlook an anonymous machine. Cover the frame around the  logo with paper first and stick the tape to itself rather than to the paintwork. That way you avoid damage to the paint when the tape is removed.

**76: Basket case.** A wicker bicycle basket is highly practical (see Tip 65) but also deeply unfashionable. Thieves are drawn to the cool and the high-tech. Fit a basket and your bike may escape their attention.

**77: Two bikes.** If you habitually park in places where there's a theft problem you might want to consider buying a cheap and unglamorous second bike, often known as a hack bike. Use it for commuting and mundane utility trips, and keep your best bike for weekends and special journeys. If the hack gets nicked it's a less heartrending experience than losing your pride and joy.

**78: Insure.** It's easy and often quite cheap to add bicycles to your household insurance policy. Some policies include bikes as a matter of course, although there's usually a fairly low limit on the value covered. Alternatively, there are specialist insurers which offer benefits such as new-for-old replacement and discounts for insuring more than one bike.

Some policies include terms and conditions that could only have been written by a weasel: the bike needs to be secured with a certain brand of lock; it has to be stored overnight in a brick or concrete building or locked to a specified type of bike stand; it won't be covered when used outside the UK; and so on. As with all insurance it pays to read the small print.

**79: Squirrel.** Rather than pay an insurance company, you might prefer to be your own insurer. Find a high-interest savings account and set up a small standing order, say £10 a month. If your bike is pinched the following week you're in trouble, but assuming it survives the year you'll have £120 (plus whatever interest you've earned) to put towards a replacement. It takes a bit of willpower – under no circumstances must you raid the account – but in the long run you'll save a sizeable amount in premiums and accumulate a substantial bike replacement fund.

# 11: Light up

There's no need to stop cycling when the sun goes down. It's as easy to ride at night as it is during the day. In fact, there are some advantages to cycling in the dark. Outside the rush hours there tends to be less traffic about, and you get a better sense of what's going on around you with cars' headlights signalling their appr‹ away. Night riding can be exhilaratin you see more of nearby objects and l‹ distant ones, so everything seems to whizzing by and it feels as if you're g faster than you actually are.

Your natural night vision together with the moonlight, and street lighting in urban areas, is usually enough to let you can see where you're going. But you still need to fit lights to your bike – because it's the law, and because they help others to see you.

**80: Battery lights.** Battery-powered bike lights are the most popular. There are three main types.

● Those with a **halogen bulb** (usually front lights) are extremely bright. Their drawback is that they are also extremely power hungry. Your batteries will be drained after just a few hours. If you use your lights morning and evening for a typical 20-minute commute you'll be buying new batteries every fortnight.

- Lights with a **filament bulb** are noticeably less bright than halogen lamps but their batteries will last at least twice as long. They're perfectly adequate unless your journey takes you through really dark places.

- **Light Emitting Diodes** (LEDs) don't project light in quite the same way the other sort of lights do, but they glow with great vigour. They can also be set to flash (see Tip 81). LEDs consume power remarkably frugally, so they need smaller batteries. I have a matchbox-sized rear LED still on its original pair of AA batteries after two years of regular use.

Whichever type of light you go for, you need to buy a clear white one for the front of your bike and a red one for the back.

**81**: **Flash.** Most LED bike lights (see Tip 80) can be set to flash as well as to deliver a continuous light. In flashing mode the lights are even more attention grabbing and the battery life is extended even further. Flashing lights were unlawful until 1995 when the law was revised. Now they're legal and you can flash with confidence.

**82**: **Recharge.** If you use battery lights (see Tip 80) they'll usually come with disposable batteries. Once these have expired, replace them with rechargeables. They cost more than normal batteries and you'll need to buy a charger, but you'll recoup the investment in no time. Rechargeable batteries can be juiced up and reused over and over again. Using them makes environmental as well as financial sense, as it reduces the number of batteries being scrapped, whether in landfill or recycled.

**83: Generate.** You can dispense with batteries altogether and generate your own electricity by using a dynamo. Dynamos used to have a major drawback in that, when you stopped cycling, they cut out, plunging you into darkness. Now however, many incorporate a 'standlight' feature, which means that your lights retain a bit of electrical charge and stay lit for a few minutes even when you're stationary.

The classic bolt-on dynamo is a bottle-shaped device which rubs against a tyre, drawing off energy and powering your lights. They're affordable (from about £15) but they have two drawbacks. One is that when pressing against the tyre they slow you down very slightly; the other is that in wet weather they can slip rather than rub and your lights go out.

The alternative is a hub dynamo. These are far more efficient and reliable. The downside is that they cost about £100 and, on top of that, you'll need to pay for them to be built into the hub of your wheel by an expert.

**84: Dress to fluoresce.** Being seen and, crucially, being recognised by others as a fellow road user is an active as well as a passive process. How you ride, where on the road you position yourself, and how you interact with others all have an effect. These are important skills and they're quite easy to learn (see Chapter 4).

That said, brightly coloured cyclists are undoubtedly easier to spot than those wearing dark clothes. And at night, or in dull weather, cyclists wearing fluorescent materials really stand out. Most cycle shops stock high-visibility clothing, some of it very tastefully styled. If you're on a budget, check out your local council's road safety department too. They often have fluorescent tabards and sashes for sale at very low prices.

**85: Reveal all.** Having fitted lights to your bike and donned a high-visibility tabard, be sure that other road users can see them. Don't wear a black rucksack over your hi-vis or let the tail of your jacket flop down over your rear light.

# 12: Maintenance

Cycle maintenance isn't glamorous. For many people it's way off their radar: too tricky; too tedious. But maintenance is important. Bikes are not crude implements like garden rollers. They're generally tough and reliable but they're sophisticated machines with many hundreds of moving parts that need regular adjustment and lubrication, and periodic replacement.

Your favourite bike shop will be pleased to service your bike for you. Just book it in. A mechanic will check everything, looking for signs of wear and tear. They'll adjust your gears and brakes, replace worn cables and brake blocks, and lubricate the parts that need it. You'll also be informed about any underlying problems likely to need attention in the near future.

But it's easy to learn a few simple maintenance skills yourself. You may find classes run by local cycling groups or by community-minded bike shops. Or you can teach yourself using books, YouTube tutorials and a bit of trial and error.

To start you off, this chapter provides a gentle initiation into basic bike maintenance. It's all straightforward stuff and, with the exception of inflating your tyres (for which you'll need a pump), no tools are required.

**86: The M-shaped check**. It's important to check your bike over periodically. I try to do it once a month or before embarking on a lengthy ride. This means looking carefully and closely at every part of the bike and trying to spot any wear or damage.

To do an effective check you need some idea of what you're looking for. If you've bought a new bike and everything is working perfectly, use that as your reference point. Regular checking will enable you to identify any faults or maintenance needs as they appear.

Cycle training instructors who sometimes have to check scores of bikes in a day have developed a method to this process: the M-shaped check.

## The M-shaped check

(You can also do this with the bike turned upside down, at which point it becomes the W-shaped check.)

- Start with the front wheel hub. The quick-release fastening or wheel nuts should be tight. The wheel should spin freely with no signs of wobbling, but it shouldn't have more than a couple of millimetres of side-to-side movement.
- Check for missing or loose spokes. When you pluck them they should make a musical twang.
- The tyre should be pumped up hard. Check it for signs of wear or cracks and splits. Remove any debris that might be stuck in the tread.
- Spin the front wheel and apply the brake. It should stop the wheel instantly and prevent it turning. Check the brake pads for signs of wear and ensure that they grip the wheel rim – they shouldn't touch the tyre. The brake cable shouldn't be frayed.
- The handlebars should turn smoothly and the handlebar stem needs to be aligned with the front fork. The stem shouldn't be raised beyond the maximum extension mark.
- Inspect the frame for signs of rust or damage.
- The pedals should spin freely and be attached tightly to the cranks. The cranks themselves should be fastened firmly to the bottom bracket with no more than a smidgeon of side-to-side movement.
- Check that the teeth of the chainring are not worn and, if there is more than one chainring, ensure that that the chain will shift easily between rings. The cable should not be frayed. Check that the chain moves freely from cog to cog. Look out for corroded or damaged chain links.

- The seatpost should be set at the correct height (never beyond its maximum extension mark) and secured tightly. The saddle should be firmly attached.
- The back brake, its cable, wheel, tyre and hub should be checked in the same way as those at the front. The gears should shift easily. The cable should be sound. The derailleur should be clean and undamaged. If there's a rear luggage rack, ensure that all fastenings are tight and that nothing rubs against the tyre.

**87: Keep it clean.** Bikes like being cleaned, and if you do it regularly – say once a month – it's a quick and even enjoyable task. Use warm soapy water. Avoid washing-up liquid and household detergents because they contain salt which will encourage rust. Bike shops sell a huge array of cleaning products together with specially shaped brushes and sponges. Alternatively, a window-cleaning sponge, an old toothbrush and a big bottle of car shampoo are cheaper and almost as good. Wash your bike, rinse it with clean water, dry it and, if you're really keen, wax it. The wax adds an attractive shine and helps prevent dirt from sticking. Remove any wax from your wheel rims and brake blocks by wiping them over with something that cuts grease (methylated spirits, vinegar or computer screen wipes all work).

**88: Oil your chain.** If it's showing signs of rust or if it makes an agonised groan as you turn the pedals, your chain is in its death throes. It's grinding away your gears and it's forcing you to pedal harder. A healthy chain is shiny and it slithers along almost silently.

There are many different types of cycle oil and any is better than none. Apply it with the bike upright. Hold a pedal, rotate the crank backwards and dribble a drop or two on to each link of the chain. Do this for a two or three complete revolutions of the entire chain until every bit is covered. If you use oil in aerosol form you need to be careful that you don't spray your wheel rims and brake blocks as well. Tape a sheet of newspaper over them. Having doused your chain with oil, hold an old rag round it and turn the chain backwards again. Use the rag to soak up the surplus oil and to work the remainder into each link.

**89: Avoid punctures.** Ah, if only! There are puncture-proof tyres on the market but they're heavy and slow. It's like swapping your running shoes for a pair of lead diving boots. Rather better are puncture resistant tyres that have a lining of Kevlar, the stuff bullet-proof vests are made from. Alternatively, you can buy strips of Kevlar and line the inside of normal tyres yourself.

Another preventative measure is to squirt a disgusting-looking liquid called Slime into the tyre's inner tube through the valve. If the tyre and tube are punctured the Slime solidifies and plugs the hole. It will fix small punctures, but larger cuts, such as from a piece of glass, are a lost cause: you'll end up with an irreparable puncture and a pool of goo.

The best approach is to buy good-quality tyres (see Tip 14) and to replace them before they're too badly worn. Keep them pumped up (see Tip 90) and inspect them regularly. Pull out any sharp bits that get lodged in the tread.

Finally, accept the fact that you'll get a puncture at some point, and have a contingency plan (see Chapter 13).

**90: Pump it up.** Even if you're lucky enough to avoid punctures, the inner tubes inside your tyres constantly leak tiny amounts of air. It's hard work riding on a soft tyre and they're more prone to wear and to punctures. If your tyres are really squashy you risk damaging the wheel.

Buy a pump and learn how to use it. There are mini-pumps, which can be carried in a pannier or pocket, and traditional longer ones that fasten to the bike. Pumps described as 'double action' deliver a blast of air into the tyre when they're pulled as well as pushed. Track pumps (sometimes called floor pumps) are for home or workshop use. They stand upright and you use both hands to push a T-shaped handle. Many cyclists carry a mini-pump for emergencies and keep a track pump back at base for serious inflation.

Check that the business end of your pump fits on to your inner tubes' valves.

There are two types of valve in common use: a thick one (called car type or Schaeder) and a thin one (called Presta). Some pumps fit only the one sort; some fit both. You can buy adaptors if you have a mismatch.

**91: Roll out the barrel (1).** With use, your bike's brake pads wear down and become less effective. Eventually, even with the levers wrenched right back until they're touching the bars, there's little or no braking force.

Bicycle brakes are quite complicated, but there's one simple adjustment that anyone can do. If your bike has straight handlebars there will be a knurled barrel-shaped knob on each brake lever. This tightens the brake cable and pulls the pads closer to the wheel rim.

To revive your brakes, turn the barrel adjuster anticlockwise. After each turn, pull the brake lever and try wheeling the bike backwards and forwards. You've got it right when you're able to lock the wheel – that is, it skids rather than turns. Now secure everything by turning the lock-ring (the knurled wheel that sits between the barrel adjuster and the lever) clockwise, until it's tight against the lever.

**92: Roll out the barrel (2).** Gears, like brakes, get a lot of use and gradually go out of alignment. Then, instead of hopping neatly from gear to gear, the chain rattles around. This is usually because the cable has stretched slightly. Now that you know what a barrel adjuster looks like (see Tip 91), you'll find it easy to put things right. Crouch down behind the bike and you'll find one sticking out from the rear derailleur.

If you're having trouble shifting down into lower gears, turn the barrel anticlockwise, towards the spokes. If you've got problems changing into higher gears, turn it clockwise.

Always move the adjuster in small increments of just half a revolution. After each, test ride the bike for a couple of minutes, shifting up and down through the gears to see if there's any improvement. If there isn't, get off and give the adjuster another half turn. Repeat until the chain shifts without hesitation.

# 13: Don't panic!

A well-maintained bicycle is a superbly reliable machine. I once cycled from Greece, into Turkey and up into Eastern Europe, eventually finishing in Prague. The total distance was 1,250 miles. My diary records two punctures and a broken gear cable (both fixed by the roadside) and two broken spokes (replaced when I got home). A colleague had an even more hassle-free journey: 4,900 miles across Canada with just four punctures. And I've known several people who've ridden from Lands End to John O'Groats with no mechanical problems whatsoever.

When things do go wrong on a bike you often get an advance warning in the form of a funny noise. Often the cause is something benign – a crisp packet trapped between mudguard and tyre, or a twig stuck in the spokes make a heck of a racket, but they're easily dislodged.

It's more serious if something has broken or worked loose, or if the noise emanates from the wheel hubs or the bottom bracket. But even then you can often effect a temporary repair with a bit of ingenuity.

This chapter suggest a few quick fixes and some more left-field strategies for those who aren't mechanically minded.

**93: Travellers' tools.** You should always carry a few bicycle tools with you. Quite what you take will depend on the sort of journey you're making. For even short hops across town I always carry a pump, a spare inner tube (see Tip 97) and a lightweight multi-tool.

## Multi-tools

These nifty, all-purpose gadgets, from the likes of Topeak and Crank Brothers, resemble Swiss army knives. Here's a typical example.

- Allen keys (eight different sizes)
- Spanners (three different sizes)
- A special spanner for removing pedals
- Flat and cross-head screwdrivers
- A chain-removing tool
- A couple of tyre levers
- A spoke key
- Bottle opener (very important!)

On a longish ride I'd add a pair of pliers and spare brake and gear cables. If I was exploring remote places, I'd also take new brake blocks, replacement spokes, a few spare chain links and a small container of cycle oil. Even if you're not able to use all these items yourself, it's still a good idea to carry them. A kind soul may stop and offer to help you (see Tip 100) and you'll be able to give them the right tools for the job.

**94**: **Bits and bobs**. Add a few extra bits and pieces to your toolkit and you'll be prepared for almost any emergency.

## Toolkit ideas

● **Zip ties** are brilliant. Originally intended for bundling electrical cables together, they work like mini lassos. I've known cyclists use them to fasten a loose bottle cage, mend a luggage rack, fix mudguards, attach a pump or a trip computer, make a key ring, repair a pannier... Most DIY shops and hardware stores sell them.

● **Masking tape** is also good for quick fixes. I've used it to patch a torn tent, repair a gash in the sidewall of a tyre and to make ad hoc sticking plaster. Turn your bike into a tape dispenser by wrapping a length round one of the tubes.

● **Superglue** will repair shoes, saddles, split tyres, glasses, cameras and cracked bike lights.

● **Dental floss** can be used to sew torn clothes, luggage or camping gear back together – thread it through a darning needle. On the bike, use it to tie down components that have worked loose or to hold a broken luggage rack together. It's amazingly versatile. You can even clean your teeth with it.

**95**: **Fix a flat.** Sooner or later, you'll get a flat tyre. The self-reliant, liberated cyclist can shrug off such misfortune, because they can whip off the wheel, remove the tyre, pull out the inner tube, find the puncture, apply a patch, put everything back together again and pump it up, in under two minutes. Actually, I take quite a bit longer – but I can do it. You can too. There are books that explain how, and you can find step-by-step instructions, for free, on the internet. You may also find that local cycling groups run courses. Or you may know a friend, relative or colleague who could teach you. Give it a go. Master puncture repair and you've learnt a vital skill.

**96**: **Clean hands.** If you have to tinker with your bike at the roadside you can prevent your hands from getting filthy by wearing disposable gloves. Keep a couple of pairs in your toolkit. Alternatively, if you prefer working ungloved, clean your hands afterwards with a baby wipe or similar moist clean-up square. Swarfega Wipes remove even the blackest grime in seconds and they moisturise your hands. (And they smell like psychedelic fruit salad!)

**97 : Fix a flat – later.** Mending punctures on the grass verge of a country lane is fine on a summer's day when time is on your side. At night, in the rain, in a dodgy part of town, you might feel rather more pressured. One option is to carry a spare inner tube with you. If you get a puncture, remove the wheel and tyre, feel around inside the tyre and remove anything sharp that's poking though, then fit your new tube. Put the tyre and wheel back on and pump it up. If you really can't get the hang of using a bicycle pump you can buy cans of compressed carbon dioxide that inflate a tyre in seconds. Then take the punctured tube home and repair it at your leisure, hot coffee to hand.

**98 : Get picked up.** The Environmental Transport Association (ETA) sees itself as the Green equivalent of the AA or the RAC. Like those organisations it provides services for motorists, but, uniquely, it also offers a roadside recovery service for cyclists. If your bike develops a problem more serious than a puncture and you're unable to complete your journey, an ETA patrol person will take you and your bike to a nearby railway station, cycle repair shop, hotel or – if feasible – back home.

**99: Taxi!** If you can't fix it yourself and you're not an ETA member (see Tip 98), call a cab instead. It's a little-known fact that most UK taxis will take bicycles. Usually there's a small additional charge. The classic black cabs or taxis based on people carriers are your best bet. Store a couple of firms' numbers in your mobile phone and, for when you're travelling further afield, keep a note of the national taxi hotline – **0871 750 3333** – it will connect you to the nearest cab company. When booking the taxi make it clear that it's for you and a bicycle.

Drivers may refuse to take your bike if its covered with mud or dripping oil, so try to spruce it up a bit while you're waiting for the cab to arrive. Of course, if you clean your bike regularly (see Tip 87) you won't have this problem!

**100: Stop a cyclist.** If you're really stuck, flag down a fellow cyclist and ask for help. In this cynical, uncaring age, when neighbours barely know each other and strangers are viewed with suspicion, there's still a surprising degree of camaraderie on the open road. Most cyclists have had a breakdown (mechanical, not nervous) at some point, and they're likely to be sympathetic to the plight of a fellow traveller. Cycle tourists or seasoned commuters (look for the fluorescent clothing, the classy bike, the bulging panniers) will probably have a full set of tools and be willing to lend you what you need. Employ strategies such as fluttering eyelashes and smiling sweetly, or looking completely gormless (my speciality) and they may even help you with the repair.

# 14: Get active

Cycling reduces traffic congestion, cuts greenhouse emissions, improves public health and, by bringing people out on to the streets and in touch with one another, makes communities friendlier and safer. On top of that, in a world where major transport projects commonly cost billions, all this can be delivered for the transport equivalent of petty cash.

Given all that it has to offer, it's staggering that we almost let cycling slip away. In Britain, cycling peaked in the early post-war years when almost everyone owned a bike and collectively rode 25 billion kilometres every year. Since then, notwithstanding the odd upward blip, the trend has been relentlessly downwards.

But suddenly, the bike is back. London, along with several other UK cities, is experiencing a spectacular growth in levels of cycling. Bike sales are buoyant. Madonna rides one. So does David Cameron and Boris Johnson. You've got one, right? Is this just another blip, or the start of a genuine cycling renaissance? To a large extent that's up to us, the UK's cyclists... We need to speak up for the bike, we need to badger the decision makers, and each of us needs to do our bit to make the world a little more cycle friendly.

**101: Improve your driving.** If someone had suggested to me when I was twenty-five years old that my driving could be improved I would have been astounded. How could one possibly improve on perfection? A few years later, when I took up cycling in a serious way, I realised that I was far from perfect and that there is a lot that drivers can do to make the cycling environment more pleasant. It's all about being considerate.

Considerate drivers slow down. When they overtake a cyclist they take care, pull right out and give them room. If they see a cyclist emerging from a side road, they wave them out. Small courtesies like this make a big difference.

**102: Join something.** The UK has two national cycling organisations, CTC and Sustrans, and most cities and large towns have a local cycle campaign. They're all working to get cycling a better deal. They raise awareness, improve infrastructure and lobby for more favourable legislation. The more supporters these groups have, the more effective they are and the more the powers-that-be sit up and take notice. Join up and add your voice.

**103: Get the BUG!** If you cycle to work, get together with a few colleagues to form a Bicycle User Group, or BUG. This is an informal group of cyclists – full-time or fair-weather, it doesn't matter – who think of ways to make the workplace more welcoming to those who travel by bike. Sometimes they organise events such as charity rides and Bike Week celebrations. The BUG idea originated in big corporations in Toronto, Canada in the 1990s. Today, they're global and there's one beetling away inside many a large organisation.

**104: Nudge, nudge.** As a cyclist you're using the greenest, cleanest and most efficient form of transport ever devised. You should expect the warmest of welcomes wherever you go. Schools, hospitals, universities and colleges, employers, retailers, rail operators... you name it, they should all be pro-cycling and make proper provision. And one day they will. Until then, it's up to individual bike users to give those in authority a nudge. Businesses value good customer relations, and elected officials are ultimately hired or fired by ordinary people.

So, write letters, make phone calls, send emails. Make your point briefly, cite facts rather than opinions, and be constructive. If you're complaining about the lack of cycle parking, for example, suggest a location where a few stands could be installed. Ask for a reply, and if you don't get one, nudge again. You're unlikely to achieve instant results, but correspondence of this sort does make a difference.

**105**: **Ride your bike!** You might not realise it, but you are someone's role model. Human beings are social creatures; they draw their ideas and their inspiration from others. You can be certain that someone seeing you riding your bike will think, 'If they can do it, maybe I could.'

You're likely to get family, friends, neighbours and work colleagues quizzing you about cycling. Why do you do it? What's it like? Can you recommend a bike shop? Take the time to answer their questions and encourage them to give cycling a try. I got my dentist on his bike that way.

As more people take to cycling, something marvellous happens. From being the preserve of cranks, athletes and hair-shirt environmentalists, cycling becomes mainstream. Drivers learn to expect bikes round every corner, and they drive more carefully and considerately. In London there was a massive 43 percent increase in cycling between 2001 and 2006, while accidents involving cyclists fell by 40 per cent. The more people cycle, the safer it is, and the more appealing it becomes.

More cycling means less traffic congestion, reduced carbon emissions, less noise, better air quality, fitter and healthier people, safer streets, vibrant neighbourhoods... Now that's the sort of world I want to live in – and I'm sure many other people do too. As a cyclist you're in the vanguard of a gentle revolution. Ride with pride! You are the future.

# Further Information

If this little book has whetted your appetite for information about cycling (and I'm delighted if it has), there are plenty of places to seek out more. This section suggests a few books, bike magazines and organisations that you're likely to find helpful. However, it is on the internet that cycling information truly abounds. If you don't have internet access at home or at work, visit your local library and they'll have you online in minutes. You'll find that, whatever aspect of cycling interests you, there are websites devoted to it and groups of enthusiasts busily discussing it.

My own modest contribution to the cycling knowledge base is **www.bike-easy.org.uk.** Naturally the site is all about urging people to buy more copies of this book, but it's also a chance to comment on all the tips listed here and to pick up exciting new tips – such as how to mend a puncture with sheep dung and a creative use for an in-flight vomit bag. Intrigued? Log on now!

## ● Magazines

**A to B magazine**
40 Manor Road, Dorchester, Dorset DT1 2AX
**T:** 01305 259998
**E:** atob@onetel.com
**W:** www.atob.org.uk
Bi-monthly magazine specialising in folding and electric bikes. Order from the publisher.

**Cycling Plus magazine**
Stocked by most of the larger newsagents
**W:** www.cyclingplus.co.uk
Monthly magazine with ideas for rides and road tests of bikes and accessories.

**Velo Vision magazine**
York Environment Centre
St. Nicholas Fields
York YO10 3EN
**T:** 01904 438224
**E:** peter@velovision.co.uk
**W:** www.velovision.com
Quarterly magazine devoted to folding bikes, recumbents and other out-of-the-ordinary cycles. Order from the publisher.

## ● Books

**Bike Repair Manual**
*Chris Sidwells, DK Adult (2004)*
Step-by-step guide to basic bike maintenance.

**Cyclecraft: The Complete Guide to Safe and Enjoyable Cycling for Adults and Children**
*John Franklin, The Stationery Office Books (2007)*
How to cycle with skill and confidence on today's roads.

**Cycling in the UK: The Official Guide to the National Cycle Network**
Nick Cotton and John Grimshaw, Sustrans (2005)
148 of the best cycle routes in the UK, including 45 selected day rides.

**The Haynes Bike Book**
*Fred Milson (ed), J H Haynes & Co (2003)*
Comprehensive guide to bike maintenance.

**On Your Bike: The Complete Guide to Cycling**
*Matt Seaton, Black Dog Publishing (2006)*
All about bicycles. Lavishly illustrated.

### Richard's 21st Century Bicycle Book
*Richard Ballantine, Pan Books (2000)*
The updated version of a classic cycling book. Slightly long in the tooth now, but still inspiring.

### Traffic-free Cycle Trails: More Than 400 Routes Around Britain
*Nick Cotton, CycleCity Guides (2004)*
Quiet bike rides on railway paths, forest trails and canal towpaths.

### Zinn and the Art of Mountain Bike Maintenance
*Lennard Zinn, VeloPress (2005)*
Illustrated guide to mountain bike maintenance, repair and troubleshooting.

All books mentioned and in print are available from www.eco-logicbooks.com

## ● Organisations

### CTC (Cyclists' Touring Club)
Parklands, Railton Road, Guildford GU2 9JX
**T:** 0870 873 0060
**E:** cycling@ctc.org.uk
**W:** www.ctc.org.uk
National cycling organisation providing a range of benefits for its members.

### Cycle Campaign Network
54–57 Allison Street, Digbeth, Birmingham B5 5TH
**W:** www.cyclenetwork.org.uk
National federation of campaigning groups. Contact them to find your local cycle campaign.

### Environmental Transport Association
68 High Street, Weybridge KT13 8RS
T:  0845 389 1010
E:  eta@eta.co.uk eta@eta.co.uk
W: www.eta.co.uk
The ecologically sound alternative to the AA or RAC. Runs a cyclists' roadside recovery service.

### Life Cycle UK
86 Colston Street, Bristol BS1 5BB
T:  0117 929 0440
E:  post@lifecycleuk.org.uk
W: www.lifecycleuk.org.uk
Free cycle maps, cycle training and other services.

### London Cycling Campaign
2 Newhams Row, London SE1 3UZ
T:  020 7234 9310
W: www.lcc.org.uk
Campaigning to make the capital more bike-friendly.

### Sustrans
National Cycle Network Centre, 2 Cathedral Square, College Green
Bristol BS1 5DD
T:  0117 926 8893
E:  info@sustrans.org.uk
W: www.sustrans.org.uk
The vision behind the National Cycle Network and other cycling projects.

## ● Websites
W: www.bike-easy.org.uk

# eco-logic books

# www.eco-logicbooks.com

eco-logic books is a small, ethically-run company that specialises in publishing and distributing books and other material that promote practical solutions to environmental problems. Those books that are still in print and mentioned in the book plus many others are available from our comprehensive website. Other topics covered include:

- Gardening and Organics
- Permaculture
- Composting
- Self Reliance
- Food and Related Issues
- Keeping Hens and other Domestic Animals
- Smallholding and Farming
- Wildlife
- Trees, Woodland Crafts and Forestry
- Orchards and Fruit Growing

- Community
- Building and Construction
- Alternative Energy
- Urban issues
- Transport
- Money and the Economy
- Trade Skills
- Sustainabilty
- Radical Thinking & Managing for Change
- Transition Thinking & Peak Oil
- Climate Change

eco logic books, Mulberry House, 19 Maple Grove, Bath BA2 3AF
Tel: 01225 484 472   Fax: 0871 522 7054
email: books@eco-logicbooks.com
web: www.eco-logicbooks.com